WASHOE COUNTY LIBRARY
3 1235 02893 8764

J
BIO
AGUILERA
2005
Duncan
-Traner

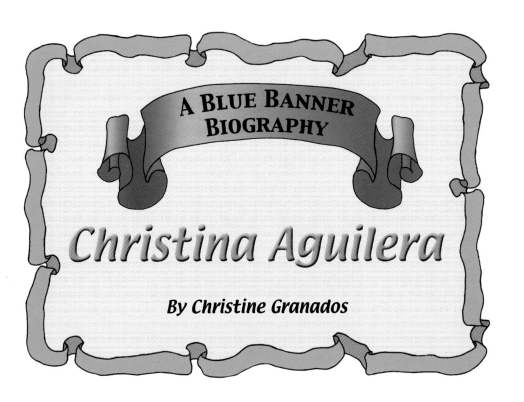

A Blue Banner Biography

Christina Aguilera

By Christine Granados

P.O. Box 196
Hockessin, Delaware 19707
Visit us on the web: www.mitchelllane.com
Comments? email us: mitchelllane@mitchelllane.com

Copyright © 2005 by Mitchell Lane Publishers. All rights reserved. No part of this book may be reproduced without written permission from the publisher. Printed and bound in the United States of America.

Printing 1   2   3   4   5   6   7   8

Blue Banner Biographies

Alicia Keys
Beyoncé
Christina Aguilera
Condoleezza Rice
Eminem
Jay-Z
Jodie Foster
Melissa Gilbert
Nelly
Rita Williams-Garcia
Rudy Giuliani
Shirley Temple

Allen Iverson
Bow Wow
Christopher Paul Curtis
Daniel Radcliffe
Eve
Jennifer Lopez
Lance Armstrong
Michael Jackson
P. Diddy
Ritchie Valens
Sally Field

Avril Lavigne
Britney Spears
Clay Aiken
Derek Jeter
Ja Rule
J. K. Rowling
Mary-Kate and Ashley Olsen
Missy Elliott
Queen Latifah
Ron Howard
Selena

Library of Congress Cataloging-in-Publication Data

Granados, Christine, 1974-
    Christina Aguilera / Christine Granados
       p. cm. — (Blue banner biography)
    Includes bibliographical references (p.), discography (p.), and index.
    ISBN 1-58415-331-8 (library bound)
    1. Aguilera, Christina, 1980—Juvenile literature. 2. Singers—United States—
Biography—Juvenile literature. I. Title. II. Series.
ML3930.A36B36 2005
782. 42164′092—dc22

2004021877

ABOUT THE AUTHOR: Christine Granados has been a writer and editor for many years. She was recently the editor of *Moderna* magazine and has been a newspaper reporter for *The El Paso Times, Austin American-Statesman,* and *Long Beach Press-Telegram*. She is a contributing author to the Contemporary American Success Stories series (Mitchell Lane), authored *Rosie O'Donnell* (Mitchell Lane) and *Sheila E.* (Mitchell Lane) and has published numerous magazine feature stories.

PHOTO CREDITS: Cover, pp. 4, 10, 14, 18 Getty Images; p. 23 Corbis; p. 26 Getty Images

ACKNOWLEDGMENTS: The following story has been thoroughly researched, and to the best of our knowledge, represents a true story. While every possible effort has been made to ensure accuracy, the publisher will not assume liability for damages caused by inaccuracies in the data, and makes no warranty on the accuracy of the information contained herein. This story has not been authorized nor endorsed by Christinia Aguilera.

Chapter 1
Perseverance 5

Chapter 2
Growing Up 9

Chapter 3
The Road to Stardom 13

Chapter 4
Her Star Continues to Rise 17

Chapter 5
Full-fledged Star 21

Chapter 6
Future: What Possibilities! 25

Chronology 29

Discography 30

For Further Reading 31

Filmography 31

Index 32

Christina dyed her hair from blonde to black. She wanted a more mature look and was tired of being a blonde.

Perseverance

Some would say Christina Aguilera has led a charmed life. Many would be envious. When she was eight years old she sang as a contestant on Star Search. At age twelve she appeared on the Disney Channel as part of the cast of The New Mickey Mouse Club. More recently, she has had the chart topping single "Beautiful;" won a *Grammy Award* for Best Pop Vocal Album for "Stripped;" and has remade the song "Car Wash" featuring Missy Elliott for the movie *Shark Tale*. Despite the busy schedule, Christina admits that she is having the time of her life. "It's definitely a dream come true," Christina said in an online chat. However, living a charmed life is not easy.

"...It's also a lot of hard work and can be draining," she said. "If you don't know already, you will quickly learn who your real friends are." For a girl who has been in the spotlight since the age of five, and has often been called 'the little girl with the big voice,' the most difficult part about stardom was living with jealousy and envy from classmates and childhood friends. Sometimes, her peers made Christina's charmed life seem cursed.

> **The difficult part of Christina's stardom was jealousy and envy from classmates and friends.**

"Going to a public school in a small town and not being around kids who did what I did made me feel like an outsider," Christina told *Rolling Stone* writer Anthony Bozza. "I even had to switch elementary schools after Star Search. The jealousy got really bad. People just felt threatened."

Christina's mother, Shelly Kearns, recalled in a *Teen People* Magazine interview, "Christina would cry every time her name got in the local paper because it meant more fear at school. We had threats of slashed tires and her getting beat up. She would be late to school because I had to time [when we were] leaving the house so that there [wouldn't be] enough time for them to do things to her. She started having nightmares so we moved."

It didn't get any better as she grew older and more famous. When she was eighteen a friend invited her to his prom and she gladly accepted. When she got to the dance the girls ignored her except to give her dirty looks. When the DJ started playing her hit song "Genie in a Bottle," the girls left the dance floor.

> "We had threats of slashed tires and her [Christina] getting beat up."

"The girls were really mean to me," Christina recalled in an interview with *The Orlando Sentinel*. "It would have been fun if they hadn't done that."

Christina has learned a valuable lesson about life through her childhood experiences — perseverance. Perseverance means sticking to something until you've accomplished your goals.

"I think that's why I became so introverted and focused on my career," she said in a *Teen People* interview. "You've got to make a decision: Are you going to go down with the situation, or are you going to focus and succeed? My dream of becoming a recording artist kept me going."

Keep going she did. Now her songs are heard on radio stations all over the United States and the world.

> ***"Are you going to go down with the situation, or are you going to focus and succeed?"***

Growing Up

Christina Aguilera was born December 18, 1980, in Staten Island, New York, to Shelly and Fausto Aguilera. Her mother, who is Irish-American, and her father, who is Ecuadorian, met in college. Her father was a U.S. Army sergeant, and as a result the family spent a lot of time traveling, from New York to Texas, New Jersey and Japan.

"I always envied people who had best friends they've known since they were little, because I've never had that," Christina told *Rolling Stone*. "I'd had to keep picking up and moving." Christina not only had to contend with moving all the time, but her parents' marriage was troubled. She told *Entertainment Weekly*, "One part of why I wanted fame so bad[ly] was to use it to spread the word about domestic violence and child abuse. It was something that I had been exposed to, and had experienced on a certain level."

Always one to make the best of a bad situation, Christina found peace in music. Her mother recalls the times fondly. "When she was two, I knew what Christina was going to do," Shelly Kearns told *Rolling Stone*. "She'd line up all of her

Christina poses for a pre-kindergarten photo taken in 1985 in Sagamihara, Japan.

stuffed animals and sing to them...I've never seen anybody so focused."

She also remembers her childhood years being filled with her parents' Spanish conversations. Her mother was a Spanish translator who nurtured her daughter's bicultural life. "I can't speak Spanish nearly as well as I can understand it, but I'm working on it," Christina told *Latina* magazine.

Her parents separated in 1985 when Christina was five years old, and she, her sister, Rachel, and her mother settled in Pennsylvania, with her grandmother Delcie Fidler.

Christina embraces her cultural heritage. Her mother makes Ecuadorian dishes she learned from her ex-mother-in-law, such as empanadas and a drink made with oatmeal, pineapple, and cinnamon that Christina loves. Christina said that the divorce and the bad times at school helped her grow and become a stronger person. "The divorce and hard times at

> *Christina embraces her cultural heritage. Her mother makes Ecuadorian dishes.*

school, all those things combined to mold me, to make me grow up more quickly. And it gave me the drive to pursue my dreams that I wouldn't necessarily have had otherwise," she told *The Washington Post*.

Pursue isn't really the word to describe Christina's ambition. She went for stardom like gangbusters. Her mother recalled, "When she was older, if there wasn't a block party or somewhere for her to sing, she'd get irritable." So her mother lined up local block parties as a place for Christina to sing, and soon the young girl was belting the national anthem at professional hockey, baseball, and football games in Pittsburgh. "I was signing autographs.... I would be sitting there printing when I barely knew how to spell my name," Christina said in a *Teen People* interview.

This was just the start of things to come.

> **Christina was belting out the national anthem at professional hockey, baseball, and football games.**

The Road to Stardom

When she was still a very young girl, Christina landed a spot as a Star Search contestant. "I was eight, and I sang Whitney Houston's 'Greatest Love of All,'" she said. She lost. "I was a good sport about it. My mom made me go back out and shake [the winner's] hand and tell him I was happy he won. Tears were running down my face. Awful," Christina told *Rolling Stone*.

Christina remembers how her celebrity status in elementary school not only hurt her but also hurt her mother. "As soon as Star Search happened, a lot of my mom's old friends, other parents, wouldn't talk to us anymore. Sometimes teachers made it difficult because I would be out with the flu, and I would return to school and the teachers would be like, 'Oh, she wasn't out sick; she was out singing somewhere,'" Christina said in a *Teen People* interview. Even the kids at school made it difficult for her: "I would make one friend and these girls would steal (her) away. It was

Christina (second row, right side) photographed with Britney Spears (front row, right side) and Justin Timberlake (3rd row, right side) in 1993 when they were in **The New Mickey Mouse Club.**

tough." However, that didn't stop Christina. She continued to sing at block parties, and she auditioned for *The New Mickey Mouse Club*. She was asked to join two years later, when producers thought she was old enough.

When she was twelve years old Christina's life changed in many ways. She became a permanent member of *The New Mickey Mouse Club* on the Disney Channel, and her mother married paramedic James Kearns. This created a larger family of Mom, Dad, Christina, Rachel, stepbrother Casey, stepsister Stephanie, and later, half brother Michael.

Christina shuttled back and forth between Orlando, Florida, where her show was taped, and her home in Wexford, Pennsylvania (near Pittsburgh). Eventually, she left Marshall Middle School in eighth grade because she felt she did not fit in; after that, she was home schooled. She was a Mouseketeer from 1993 until 1994 with other

> *Christina's life changed when she became a member of the Mickey Mouse Club.*

young talented artists such as Britney Spears and Justin Timberlake. "Being in *The Mickey Mouse Club* was a really, really good experience for me," she said on an America Online chat. "First of all, because of the experience, [I was] able to show three different sides of [my]self: [my] acting ability, dancing ability, and vocal ability. Because it was a variety show for kids, you have to know how to do all three. It was good exercise. And, second of all, [I loved] working with [the] other kids on the show, so many other kids on the show, a cast of twenty that truly enjoyed performing and saw it as a future career choice as much as I did. It was really, really cool to be able to be with other kids that could relate to those dreams of mine and that passion and that love for music and film as much as I did." After her experiences with the other kids in public school, this was a much happier time for Christina.

> *It was really, really cool to be able to be with other kids that could relate to those dreams of mine..."*

Her Star Continues to Rise

After two years on the weekly Disney show, Christina traveled to Japan to record the duet "All I Wanna Do" with Japanese pop singer Keizo Nakanishi. She caused a near riot at the Golden Stag Festival in Transylvania, Romania, when she sang two songs in front of a crowd of 10,000 people.

When she returned home, Christina's manager, Steve Kurtz, asked her to record a demo (an audition tape). She recorded the tape on a stereo in her living room singing to a karaoke tape of Whitney Houston's "I Wanna Run to You." Ron Fair, the senior vice president at RCA (record company) liked Christina's tape. He asked to meet with her. "I [had] a meeting with Christina and said, 'Okay, sing!' It was in a very, very small office, with three or four people crammed into it, but she basically got into that performance zone and sang a cappella (with no accompanying music), with a complete sense of self-possession, with perfect intonation," he told *The Washington Post*. "She was very determined and extremely professional. From a musical point of view [she] was way beyond her years and it was obvious that she had the potential to become a major vocalist. I went to my boss and said, 'This girl's the bomb, let's sign her.'"

> "From a musical point of view [she] was way beyond her years and it was obvious that she had the potential..."

RCA did sign a contract with Christina. She was signed the very same week she was chosen to sing "Reflections" for the Disney animated movie *Mulan*. The song, which was released in 1998, became a Top 15 single and was nominated for a Golden Globe Award for Best Original Song in a Motion Picture. Building on her success with "Reflections," RCA spent $1 million on writers, producers, voice lessons, and marketing for Christina. They marketed her in a different way than they had done for any other artist. They used the internet to ensure that Christina's name would get out to the right people — teenagers. A company called Electric Artists hired workers to surf the net and create a buzz about Christina. The people at Electric Artists posted information on

Christina (center), her sister Rachel (left), and her mother Shelly Kearns (right) photographed at the 1st Annual Latin Grammy Awards in 2000.

message boards on such web sites as www.alloy.com and other hip teen sites like www.gurl.com. They visited chat rooms and talked about Christina, and they even asked America Online to do features on Christina. They talked up Christina's first single, "Genie in a Bottle," so much that the song entered the *Billboard* charts at No. 1 and stayed on the Hot 100 for five weeks. The second single, "What a Girl Wants," released from her first album, titled *Christina Aguilera*, reached No. 1 on the *Billboard* Hot 100 in the year 2000. The album went platinum, which means it sold over 1 million copies.

> *Christina's first single, "Genie in a Bottle" entered the Billboard charts at No. 1.*

Full-fledged Star

The popularity of her debut album helped Christina get Grammy nominations for Best New Artist and Best Female Pop Vocal Performance. In May 2000 Christina won the Grammy for the Best New Artist. She was so stunned that in her acceptance speech she said, "Oh my God, you guys. I seriously do not have a speech prepared whatsoever. I'm shaking right now."

After she had calmed down a bit, she talked to her fans on an America Online chat and recalled, "Winning the Grammy was truly incredible. I had dreamt about actually winning a Grammy since I was, oh, seven or eight years old. Best New Artist is funny enough: that happened to be the category

I looked at hoping one day to at least be nominated for. I mean I didn't expect it whatsoever, just because my album had been out the shortest amount of time out of everyone I was up against, but was shocked, completely shocked and overwhelmed. The greatest moment careerwise to date."

Since her 2000 Grammy victory Christina has been busy performing around the world. The announcement for the "Justified and Stripped Tour" with Justin Timberlake started rumors that Christina and Justin were dating. Her office website, www.christinaaguilera.com says those rumors are false. "They are touring together, but there is no romance. They've been good friends since they were about 11 years old, and still are. But there is only a working relationship, not a romantic one."

As a matter of fact, Christina has been linked to many handsome young men, such as Enrique Iglesias, Ricky Martin, MTV's Carson Daly, and even Prince William.

She talked to her online fans on her web site about love and her first kiss. "My first kiss was when I was really little because I would kiss boys just for fun. My first boyfriend kiss was when I was thirteen. As to love, I know that I have cared a lot about certain people. As to that completely head-over-heels person I want to be with forever, I have yet to experience that." She does admit that she gets crushes on celebrities, but she has no time for a boyfriend in her life.

Since the release of her first album, she has been asked to perform on Saturday Night Live, The Tonight Show with Jay Leno, The Late Show

Christina performs during the 2000 American Music Awards in Los Angeles.

with David Letterman, MTV's Total Request Live, The *Essence* Awards, Disney Summer Jams, and The World Music Awards.

Christina barely has time to rest. Aside from performing she also has interview requests from *Entertainment Weekly, People, Latina, Hispanic, Interview,* and *Rolling Stone* magazines. Awards and honors also fill her schedule. Christina hosted the 2003 MTV European Music Awards in Edinburgh, Scotland. Not only was it an honor to host this awards show but she was also won the Best Female Artist award. In 2004, the fashion magazine *Glamour* honored Christina as "Woman of the Year."

> *In 2004, the fashion magazine Glamour honored Christina as "Woman of the Year."*

Future: What Possibilities!

With 20 million album sales under her belt, the future holds limitless possibilities for Christina. She made her acting debut in the animated movie *Shark Tale*. Christina talked to BBC Radio 1 about her role as a jellyfish. "It was really funny, it was the take-off of a certain look I guess. I could say closest to when I had braids, which was at the Grammys four years ago [2000]. So it was really interesting and really funny. When I first saw those big, bright eyes and those braids. I'm a jellyfish and it was really really funny. It was my first film debut in a way."

Not only was Christina in the movie, she also recorded a song for the soundtrack. Collaborating

Christina attends the **Shark Tale** *premiere in September 2003 in New York City.*

with Missy Elliot they remade the disco hit "Car Wash." The pair also worked together on the *Moulin Rouge* soundtrack. Christina has worked with other recording artists such as Ricky Martin, Pink, Mya, 'Lil Kim, and Nelly.

Christina has also found time to support charities. She donated $200,000 to the Women's Center and Shelter of Greater Pittsburgh in Oakland, Pennsylvania. While speaking at the shelter Christina said, "I'm so happy and proud to be a part of this. It feels good to be in the room with all these people who have donated all their time to this...I always thought that if I was ever in a position to make a difference, I wanted to do something to help." She also made a difference when she lent her hands to the charity organization Precious Impressions. An autographed statue of Christina's hands were auctioned off on eBay with the proceeds benefiting the Crisis Center for women and children of abuse

> *Christina has worked with other recording artists such as Ricky Martin, Pink, Mya, 'Lil Kim, Missy Elliott, and Nelly.*

in Utah. Other charities she support are the Family Crisis Center in Los Angeles, the National Coalition for Domestic Violence, the National Alliance of Breast Cancer Organizations, and the Defenders of Wildlife.

What can we expect from Christina in the future? Her life is unpredictable and her talent provides her with endless possibilities for the future. Whatever she decides, you can bet she will make it a success through her hard work and perseverance.

> *Her life is unpredictable and her talent provides her with endless possibilities for the future.*

CHRONOLOGY

1980 Born December 18, Staten Island, New York; father: Fausto; mother: Shelly
1985 Parents divorce
1988 Appears as a contestant on *Star Search*
1990 Sings the national anthem at professional baseball, football, and hockey games
1992 Becomes a Mouseketeer on *the New Mickey Mouse Club*
1998 Records "Reflection" for the Disney animated film *Mulan*; signs with RCA to record an album
1999 Releases self-titled album and the single "Genie In A Bottle." Both the album and the single go platinum.
2000 Second hit with "What a Girl Wants." Wins Best New Artist Award at the Grammy's and Best New Female Artist at the World Music Awards. Releases Spanish language album *Mi Reflejo* and holiday album *My Kind of Christmas*
2001 Records the single "Nobody Wants to Be Lonely" with Ricky Martin and remakes "Lady Marmalade" with Mya, Pink, and 'Lil Kim. Both singles were hits on the Top 40 *Billboard* charts
2002 Christina wins her second Grammy for Best Pop Collaboration with Vocals for "Lady Marmalade." Her album, *Stripped*, is released in October.
2003 Christina tours with Justin Timberlake.
2004 Wins her third Grammy Award for Best Female Pop Vocal Performance for her song, "Beautiful."

DISCOGRAPHY

Albums
1999 *Christina Aguilera*
2000 *Mi Reflejo*
My Kind of Christmas
2001 *Just Be Free*
2002 *Stripped*

Singles
1998 *Reflection*
1999 *Genie in a Bottle*
The Christmas Song (Chestnuts Roasting on an Open Fire)
What A Girl Wants
2000 *I Turn to You*
Come on Over (All I Want Is You)
Just Be Free
2001 *Nobody Wants to Be Lonely (duet with Ricky Martin)*
Lady Marmalade (with 'Lil Kim, Pink, and Mya)
What's Going On (All Star Tribute to 9/11)
Pero Mi Acuredo de Ti
Falsas Esperanzas
2002 *Dirrty*
2003 *Beautiful*
Fighter
Can't Hold Us Down
The Voice Within

Books

Dominguez, Pier. *Christina Aguilera: A Star is Made: The Unauthorized Biography*. Amber Books, 2002.

Marin, Maggie. *Christina Aguilera*. Universe Publishing, 2000.

Websites

Christina Aguilera

    http://www.christinaaguilera.com

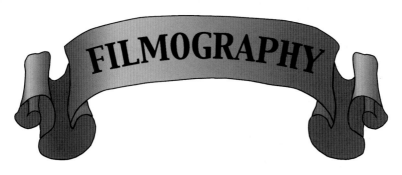

DVD/Videos

1999 *My Reflection*

2000 *Genie Gets Her Wish (Unauthorized Biography)*

2004 *Stripped Live in the UK*

Movies

2004 *Shark Tale*

INDEX

Aguilera, Christina
   2003 MTV European Music
      Awards   24
   birth of   9
   "Beautiful"   5
   charities   27-28
   collaborating 27
   "Genie in a Bottle"   7, 19
   2000 Best New Artist
      Grammy   21-22
   New Mickey Mouse Club, The
      5, 15-16
   performances   23-24
   "Reflections" 18-19
   Star Search   13
   "What a Girl Wants"   20
   "2004 Woman of the Year"
      Award   24

Aguilera, Fausto (father)   9
Aguilera, Rachel (sister)   11
Christina Aguilera (album)   20
Electric Artists   19-20
Elliott, Missy   5, 27
Fidler, Delcie (grandmother)   11
Kearns, Casey (stepbrother)   15
Kearns, James (stepfather)   15
Kearns, Shelly (mother) 6, 10
Kearns, Stephanie (stepsister)
   15
Kearns, Michael (half brother)
   15
Kurtz, Steve   17
Fair, Ron   17-18
Nakanishi, Keizo   17
RCA   17-20
Shark Tale 5, 25